Create your Future

by

Motivation Joy

HOW TO RAISE PEOPLE'S MENTAL AND PHYSICAL STANDARDS TO IMPROVE THEIR LIVES

CONTENTS

COPYRIGHT

INTRODUCTION

Choosing to consciously create your future is one of the most important things you can do to improve your life. Do you have any idea about what you would like to create as a future?

Sadly, not too many people take the time to look at what they would like to create as their future. They just want their life to continue to be better but never set a clear target for themselves in their life. That is not creating a future. It's essential for you to think about where you want to be, whether it's in one month, one year, or one decade from today. Taking the time to determine where you want to create and to be is the best way to make sure you are going in the right direction and help you avoid creating a life that doesn't excite you.

Those who don't have a clue about what they would like to create as their future may not believe that they have any control over their lives. They wander through life heavily influenced by the people and circumstances that surround them. They give their power over to the environment rather than using it to create the life they genuinely desire. This results in them achieving less than what are they capable of.

Choosing to take charge your future is one of the best choices you can make in your life. Knowing what you would like to create as your future will allow you to tap into your intrinsic abilities and put you on the right path for uncovering your hidden power.

Knowing what you would like to create as your future gives direction to your subconscious mind, helping you to create the life you desire. It gives you a path in life. However, having vague desires like "I want to make more money," or "I want to live a happy life," won't end up leading you to a fulfilling life.

Your subconscious mind behaves similarly to GPS; it is continuously scanning the environment around you for the information relevant to the details you've given it. This is why knowing what you would like to create as your future will provide you with a higher chance of accomplishing them. A strong signal is sent to your subconscious mind, allowing it to unleash its power of awareness to receive new and different possibilities and open the doors to everything you are capable of.

Are you creating your own future or are you leaving it in the hands of others, or to fate? If you expand your ability to be aware of future possibilities, you will know what's required in the future. You still have a choice as to whether or not you create it.

CHAPTER ONE

YOUR POTENTIAL IS UNLIMITED

"If one advances confidently in the direction of his dreams and endeavors to live the life he has imagined, he will meet with a success unexpected in common hours." (Henry David Thoreau)

Your mind has all the power you need to get you anything you really want in life. Your ability to harness the incredible creative and constructive capacities of your thinking determines everything that happens to you. When you unlock your mental powers, you will accomplish more in a few months than many people do in several years.

Thought Is Creative

Perhaps the most important corollary of the Law of Cause and Effect is this: "Thoughts are causes, and conditions are effects."

Your mind is the most powerful force in your universe. You are where you are and what you are because of your habitual ways of thinking. Your thoughts are creative, and they ultimately create your reality. As Emerson said, "A man becomes what he thinks about most of the time." Therefore, if you change your thinking, you change your life. You actually become a different person and get different results.

The greatest thinkers of all time, dating back to the earliest religions, philosophers and metaphysical schools, have all emphasized the power of the human mind to shape individual destiny.

—

Become A Magnet For Good Luck

The Law of Attraction explains perhaps the most important luck factor of all. This law, first written about 3000 years before Christ, says that, "You are a living magnet, and you inevitably attract into your life the people, circumstances, ideas and resources in harmony with your dominant thoughts."

The Law of Attraction falls under the Law of Cause and Effect. The Law of Attraction explains almost every circumstance of your life. People who think and talk continually about what they want seem to attract more and more of those very things into their lives. People who talk about what they don't want, or the things they fear or worry about, or who are angry and resentful, continually attract negative and unhappy experiences into their lives as well.

The Law of Attraction is neutral, as are all of these other laws and principles. Natural laws do not play favorites. They function automatically and unemotionally. They affect you either positively or negatively, depending on whether you use them constructively or destructively.

Perhaps the most important lesson you will ever learn is this: to be successful and happy, you must think and talk only about the things you want. At the same time, you must discipline yourself not to think and talk about the things you don't want. This may sound simple and obvious, but it is often the most difficult of all exercises in self-control and self-mastery.

You Will See It When You Believe It

The Law of Belief is another luck factor that you can use to your advantage. The Law of Belief states that, "Whatever you believe, with conviction, becomes your reality."

William James of Harvard wrote that, "Belief creates the actual fact." In the New Testament it says, "According to your faith, it is done unto you." In the Old Testament it reads, "As a man thinketh (or believeth) in his heart, so is he." Throughout all of history, people have recognized that our beliefs play a major role in the way we see the world, and in the way we think and behave.

If you absolutely believe that you are destined to be a great success in life, you will think and behave accordingly, and you will make it come true. If you confidently believe that you are a lucky person, and that good things are continually happening to you, your belief will become the actual fact of your life.

You See What You Already Believe

Once upon a time, two shoe salesmen, from different companies, were sent to an African country to explore the market for shoes. The first shoe salesman hated the assignment and wished he didn't have to go. The second shoe salesman loved the assignment and saw it as a great opportunity for advancement in his company.

When they each arrived in the African country, they studied the local market for shoes. They then both send telegrams back to their head offices. The first salesman, who didn't want to be there, wrote, "Trip has been wasted. No market in this country. Nobody wears shoes."

The second salesman, who saw this as a real opportunity and believed that he could make something of it, said in his telegram, "Wonderful trip. Market opportunities unlimited. No one wears shoes."

You Create Your Own Reality

There is a short poem that says, "Two men looked out through prison bars. One saw the mud, the other saw the stars."

Shakespeare wrote that, "Nothing is but thinking makes it so."

Your beliefs do become your realities. The Law of Mind, a corollary of the Law of Belief, says that, "Thoughts objectify themselves. Thoughts held in mind produce after their kind." The results of your habitual ways of thinking eventually appear in the world around you. All you have to do is to look around you to see the truth of these timeless principles.

By Their Fruits

—

In the New Testament, Jesus says, "By their fruits, ye shall know them." You can tell what a person thinks about most of the time by looking at the fruits of his or her life. A happy, healthy, prosperous person with good friends and family is invariably a person who thinks about his life in positive terms - most of the time. He absolutely believes that happy and success are in the natural order of things for him.

Harvard University did a study a few years ago and made three predictions for that year. These predictions, as it turns out, seemed to be true for every year thereafter. The Harvard study predicted that first, in the coming year, there will be more changes than ever before. Second, in the coming year, there will be more competition than ever before. Third, in the coming year there will be more opportunities than ever before. The fourth conclusion, which was contained in a footnote, said that those who do not adjust to the rapid rate of change, respond to the increase in competition or take advantage of the new opportunities available will be out of their jobs within two years.

The Opportunities of Tomorrow

The truth about opportunities is that there are more of them today than ever before, but they are different from the opportunities of the past. There are more opportunities for more people to achieve more of their goals of health, happiness and financial independence today than have ever existed in all of human history. But to take advantage of them, you will have to adjust and adapt to the new realities of your situation, whatever they are.

One of the greatest luck factors of all, which few people realize or appreciate, is the factor of being born and living today in our world as it exists at this moment. Most of the major illnesses have been eliminated, there are no major wars or revolutions, inflation is under control, unemployment is down and the possibilities for positive, creative people are virtually unlimited.

We are entering into the Golden Age that has been dreamed about throughout all of human history. Your goal must be to take full advantage of all the wonders of the modern world to design and create your own future.

Of course, there will always be social, political and economic problems to contend with. The problems of world terrorism create new feelings of uncertainty and insecurity. But these ups and downs are inevitable. They are challenges that we will rise to, and eventually meet successfully. The good news is that for you, the possibilities are unlimited.

There Are No Limits

Your greatest limits are not external. They are internal, within your own thinking. They are contained in your personal "self-limiting beliefs." These are the beliefs that act as the brakes on your potential. These are the beliefs that cause you to sell yourself short, and to settle for far less than you are truly capable of.

Many people think that they are not smart enough, creative enough, or talented enough to get the things they want. But the fact is that most of these beliefs have no basis in reality. They are simply not true. There are very few limits on what you can really accomplish, except the ones you accept in your own mind. As Henry Ford said, "If you believe you can do a thing, or you believe you cannot, in either case, you are probably right."

Here is an important point. You cannot intensely desire something without having simultaneously the ability to attain it. The existence of the desire itself is usually proof that you have within you everything you need to fulfill that desire. Your job is simply to find out how to do it. Your job is to identify all the things that you can do to increase the probabilities and improve the averages that you will achieve your goal as you desire it, and on schedule.

Expect The Best

The Law of Expectations contains and explains another luck factor. This law says that, "Whatever you expect, with confidence, becomes your own self-fulfilling prophecy."

Perhaps the most powerful and predictable motivator of all is an attitude of positive expectations. People are most motivated to act when they are convinced that their actions will lead to a successful, positive outcome. They take action because they confidently expect good things to happen as a result of what they do.

One way to manufacture your own mental force field of positive expectations is to start off each morning by saying; "I believe something wonderful is going to happen to me today!" Repeat this affirmation several times until your entire mind is charged up with confident expectancy. "I believe something wonderful is going to happen to me today."

At the end of the day, do a brief review and think over the events of the past few hours. You will be amazed to notice the great number of wonderful things, large and small, that actually did happen to you when you mind was supercharged with this power of confident expectation.

Successful people are characterized by this attitude of positive self-expectancy. They expect to succeed more often than they fail. They expect to win more often than they lose. They expect to gain something from every experience. They look for the good in every situation. They see the glass as half full rather than as half empty. Even when things go wrong for them, they look into the temporary setback or reversal for the lessons they can learn and the advantages they can gain from the experience.

Use All Your Mental Powers

Your subconscious mind can be another luck factor, when you use it correctly. The Law of Subconscious Activity says: "Whatever thought or goal you accept in your conscious mind will be accepted by your subconscious mind as a command or instruction."

Your subconscious mind, the sending station of the power of attraction, once programmed with your goals, will then begin drawing into your life the people and resources you need to achieve them. Your subconscious mind will make your words and actions fit a pattern consistent with your self-concept, with your dominant thoughts and ideas about yourself. Your subconscious mind will determine your body language and the ways that you interact with other people. The commands you have given to your subconscious mind by your habitual ways of thinking will affect your tone of voice, your energy levels, your enthusiasm and your attitude.

Your subconscious mind is extraordinarily powerful. It works 24 hours per day. Once you begin using it in achieving your goals, you will begin to move forward at a speed that you cannot now imagine.

Activate Your Reticular Cortex

In your brain, there is a small finger-like organ called the "reticular cortex." This reticular cortex is like a telephone switchboard that accepts and forwards calls from the outside. Your reticular cortex takes in information and passes it on to your conscious mind, as well as to your subconscious mind. Your reticular cortex, or reticular activating system, works on the basis of commands that you have given it regarding what you want and what is most important to you.

For example, if you decide that you want a red sports car, you will begin to see red sports cars everywhere. This desire or goal will activate your reticular cortex and make your mind highly sensitive to red sports cars. You will become aware of red sports cars wherever you go. You will see them turning corners and parked in driveways. You will notice pictures and advertising for red sports cars. And you will attract people and ideas that will help you to finally acquire a red sports car. Was there ever anything you really wanted for a long time that you didn't eventually get, often in the most amazing way?

CHAPTER TWO

CLARITY IS CRITICAL

"The greatest thing that a man can do in this world is to make the most possible out of the stuff that has been given him. This is success and there is no other." (Orison Swett Marden)

Perhaps the most important of all luck factors is knowing exactly what you want, in each area of your life. The primary reason for great success is clear, specific, measurable goals and plans, written down and accompanied by a burning desire to accomplish them. Knowing what you want dramatically increases the probabilities that you will get it.

The primary reason for under achievement and failure is fuzziness and confusion about goals. Failure comes from the inability to decide exactly what you want, what it will look like, when you want it, and how you will attain it. As motivational speaker Zig Ziglar says, the great majority of people are "wandering generalities" rather than "meaningful specifics." The fact is that you can't hit a target that you can't see. If you don't know where you're going, you will probably end up somewhere else. You have to have goals.

A person without goals is like a ship without a rudder, carried whichever way the tides and wind are blowing. A person with clear, specific goals is like a ship with a rudder, sailing straight and true to its destination.

It is amazing how fast you change your luck by becoming intensely goal-oriented. As a wealthy friend of mine once said, "Success is goals, and all else is commentary." Goals may not be the only reason for success, but no success is possible without them!

There Are No Coincidences

Some people believe in coincidences. They believe in the power of random events to make and shape a person's life. But the fact is that in most cases, coincidences don't just happen. They can almost always be traced back to previous events and mental preparation, as explained earlier in this book.

Rather than coincidences, there are instead a variety of different probabilities that particular events will occur. According to the Law of Averages, if you try enough different things, like billiard balls rolling around the table, one or two of them are going to bang into each other. But this coming together of different events is based on law, not luck or coincidence.

Look For Serendipity In Everything

There are two important principles that are essential luck factors, and have been so throughout history. The most successful men and women experience them regularly. An understanding of these principles can open your eyes to potentials and possibilities that you may have never understood or been aware of in the past.

The first of these luck factors is the principle of "Serendipity." Serendipity has been best described as the "capacity for making happy discoveries along the road of life." The principle of Serendipity comes from the fairy tale of the three princes of Serendip. These three princes traveled around, coming upon experience after experience of misfortune and seeming disaster in the lives of others. But as a result of their visit, and the happy discoveries they made, the disaster or tragedy was turned into to greater success and happiness than before.

On one occasion, the three princes came to a farmhouse where an unfortunate accident had taken place. The farmer's only son had been thrown from the farmer's only horse and broken his leg. The horse had then run off and could not be found. The farmer was quite distressed but the three princes told him not to worry, "It's too soon to judge; something good will happen."

This country happened to be involved in a war at that time with a neighboring country. The next morning, a squad of soldiers arrived at the house to forcefully conscript all young, able-bodied men into the army. As it happened, the farmer's only son had a broken leg so he was spared from conscription.

Later that day, representatives of the government came by to seize all horses that could be used by the army. But since their only horse had run off, again the farmer was spared. Later, the army lost a great battle and most of the men and horses were killed. What appeared to be an unfortunate event, the breaking of the leg and the running off of the horse, turned out to be the saving of the farmer.

Some time later, after the war, the horse came home on its own accord, leading several other wild horses. The son's leg soon mended. And the farmer was happy. An apparent disaster turned out to be a series of blessings in disguise. This sort of thing will happen to you as well, over and over, if you allow it and you look for it.

In another story, the three princes of Serendip came across a wealthy landowner whose entire estate had been washed away by a flood. Everything he had accumulated in his lifetime was destroyed. As you can imagine, he was distraught and depressed. But the three princes of Serendip convinced him that something good would turn up.

As they walked across the land where all the soil had been washed away by the flood, they found a precious stone, and then another and another. It turned out that the flood had revealed countless precious stones that made the landowner wealthier than he had ever imagined.

Develop An Attitude of Positive Expectancy

The key to understanding serendipity is the principle of positive expectations. This principle says that the more confidently you expect something good to happen, the more likely it is to occur. The one common denominator of a serendipitous event is that it only occurs when you are completely confident that all will work out for the best, and when you are looking for something good in every setback or difficulty. Then surprisingly, all kinds of happy occurrences take place, many of which initially appear as failures or unfortunate events. They later turn out to be exactly what needed to happen for you to achieve your ultimate goal.

Your Current Situation Is Exactly What You Need

Here is an important philosophical principle: Your situation today is exactly what you need, at this moment, for your own personal growth and development. Every part of your life is exactly as it should be. Every difficulty you are facing or dealing with today contains within it possibilities that you can turn to your own advantage to achieve the kind of life that you want for yourself.

You may be working for a difficult boss in an industry where the competition is fierce, the margins are low and your potential future seems limited. If you are not careful, you may become negative about your job, and worry about your current situation. But if you realize that, according to the principle of Serendipity, it is exactly what you need at this moment, you can look into it for the benefit or advantage it might contain.

You can ask yourself, "If I was not doing this job, knowing what I now know about the job and its future, would I get into this field in the first place?" If your answer is "No," then your next question could be, "If I could do anything I really wanted, what would it be?"

Whatever it is, you can use your current experience as a springboard to higher and better experiences rather than just sitting there, wishing and hoping that things will improve. You only learn the right course for you by following the wrong course temporarily.

Think About the Future

Another luck factor is explained in the rule that "It doesn't matter where you are coming from; all that really matters is where you are going."

The past is dead. It cannot be changed. It serves only to give you guidance and wisdom so that you can make better decisions in the future. All that matters is where you are going from this moment forward. You can't allow yourself to cry over spilled milk. Look upon the past as a "sunk cost," as an investment in your life that is irretrievable. You can't get it back. Then, focus your attention on the future horizon of your own possibilities and begin moving in that direction.

The Principle of Synchronicity

This timeless principle explains perhaps the most important luck factor of all. It is intertwined and connected with many of the other principles in this book. It has been known about for thousands of years and is called "Synchronicity." It actually goes above and beyond, and works on a different plane, than the Law of Cause and Effect.

The Law of Cause and Effect says that every effect in your life has certain specific causes which you can relate to each other. The principle of Synchronicity on the other hand says that things will happen in your life that have no direct cause-effect relationship. Synchronicity happens when events that occur in your life are linked not by causality, but by meaning. There will be no direct or discernible connection between events except for the meaning they have in relation to one of your goals.

A Hawaiian Vacation

For example, imagine that you get up one morning and talk with your spouse about nice it would be to take a vacation to Hawaii. But you know you can't afford it and you couldn't get the time off anyway. Nonetheless, the idea of going to Hawaii is very attractive to you. It stimulates your mind. Your emotions of desire and interest are aroused by the idea of a Hawaiian vacation.

Any thought you emotionalize, including the idea of going to Hawaii, is passed from your conscious mind to your subconscious mind, the seat of the law of attraction. As a result, you begin to send out positive vibrations that start to attract into your life people and circumstances that will make that thought a reality. You begin to activate the principle of synchronicity.

You go to work that day fantasizing about someday taking a trip to Hawaii with your spouse. Completely unexpectedly, your boss calls you in a couple of hours later and tells you that, since you've been doing such a great job, and that now the company is in the slow season, there will be no problem if you wanted to take a week or two off as your vacation.

At lunchtime, a friend of yours tells you about a new travel agency that puts together Hawaiian vacation packages, including hotel, airfare and ground transportation, at really great prices. In fact, your friend has a brochure that has a description of exactly the island that you wanted to visit and a hotel that would be ideal for you. And the price is less than $2000 for both of you for an entire week in Hawaii.

That night, you get home and there is an income tax refund in the mail for an unexpected overpayment that amounts to, you guessed it, about $2000!

Notice what has happened. You had a very clear, emotionally charged idea of taking a trip to Hawaii with your spouse. That day, three events occurred, none of them having any connection with each other, but all of which worked together to enable you to achieve your goal in less than one day.

Get Yourself Into the Zone

This sort of synchronous event will begin to happen to you regularly once you get into the "zone." When you emotionalize your mind, clarify your thoughts, intensify your desires and approach your life with an attitude of confident, positive expectations, all sorts of serendipitous and synchronous events begin to occur in your life. The only relationship that these events have to each other is the meaning that you give them by the thoughts you think.

Alas, if your thoughts are fuzzy, confused and contradictory, these principles cannot work for you. This lack of clarity is the primary reason that most people are unhappy and unsuccessful. They have enormous potential powers but they are failing to use them to their best advantage because they don't understand how they work.

Getting A Better Job

Here's another example of synchronicity, a true story. A friend of mine was unhappy in his job. He and his wife talked about how much better off he would be if he could get a better job in a different field. They discussed his wanting to work for a smaller company where there were more opportunities for pay and promotion based on merit, rather than a rigid salary structure that put a ceiling on what he could earn.

The next night they went out for dinner at a nice restaurant. But the restaurant was full and they had lost his reservation. So instead of going home, they went to a nearby restaurant that had one table free. At the next table was a friend of his that he hadn't seen for some time. This friend and his wife were having dinner with another couple. The male member of the other couple was the president of a rapidly growing business in town. They had just been talking about how hard it was to find ambitious people who were looking for opportunity rather than security. They began chatting from table to table, and the first thing that the young man said was that he was looking for a job that had greater opportunities for advancement.

The president gave him his business card and asked him to call the following week. He called, made an appointment, went through an interview process and got the job. A year later he was earning twice as much. He and his wife had moved to a nicer home, bought a new car, and were living a much better life.

Most people would say that this was an example of "luck." But you know by now that it was an example of synchronicity. The young man was clear, confident and optimistic about what he wanted. As a result, he triggered a series of forces in the universe that not only canceled one reservation and opened another, but also sat him at exactly the right table next to the right person, at the right time who had the right opportunity for him at that time of his life.

CHAPTER THREE

KNOWLEDGE IS POWER

"Blessed is the man who finds wisdom, the man who gains understanding, for she is more profitable than silver and yields better returns than gold. She is more precious than rubies; nothing you desire can compare with her." (Bible, Proverbs 3:13-15)

There is a race on today and you are in it. The only question is whether or not you are going to win or lose. And this is largely up to you. One advantage you have is that the great majority of people aren't aware that they are in a race. They are simply strolling along. They don't know understand how competitive our world is today, is and they don't realize how important it is to win.

There is a story from East Africa that makes this point. Every morning on the Serengeti Plains of Africa, a gazelle awakes. The gazelle knows that in the day ahead, he must run faster than the fastest lion if he wants to survive. And every morning on the Serengeti Plains, a lion awakes. The lion knows that he must run faster than the slowest gazelle if he wants to eat that day.

The moral of the story is that, whether you see yourself as a gazelle or a lion, when the sun comes up, you'd better be running.

Join The Information Age

It took 6,000 years of recorded history for man to move from the agricultural age into the industrial age, which officially began about 1815. By 1950, the majority of workers in the developed countries were industrial workers. But by 1960, in less than 150 years, the industrial age was over. We had entered into the service age. There were more people working delivering services of all kinds than there were in manufacturing.

By the late 1980's, just twenty years later, we had left the service age, in terms of employment, and we had entered into the Information Age. There were more people working in the generation and processing of information than in any other area. As we move into the 21st century, we are already in the Communications Age. There are now more people employed in the generation and communication of information, ideas, entertainment, news or education, than there are employed in any other single industry.

Just imagine! It took 6,000 years to go through the Agricultural Age, 150 years to pass through the Industrial Age, 20 years to move through the Service Age, twenty more years to pass through the Information Age, and we are now in the Age of Communication.

We have gone from muscle power to mind power, from brute power to brainpower. We have evolved from a focus on making and moving things to a focus on the creation and dissemination of ideas and knowledge. For the rest of your life, the knowledge content of your work, and your ability to communicate it, is largely going to determine the value of what you do, the amount of money you earn and the overall quality of your life.

The Primary Source of Value

According to Moore's Law in computers, information processing capacity doubles every eighteen months. At the same time, the cost of information processing drops by 50%. This is a staggering increase in efficiency! If the cost and efficiency of a new Lexus automobile had improved at the same rate as the improvement in computing capacity, a new Lexus today would cost $2.00, get 700 miles per gallon of gas and travel at 500 miles per hour. In fact, a new Lexus automobile today has more computer systems in it than the Apollo 13, which was the most advanced moon rocket of its time.

In a new automobile today, more money is spent on the electronics, the knowledge and information systems that run it, than is spent on steel.

We have moved into the Information Age so quickly, with knowledge as the primary source of value, that most of the major institutions of society have not yet caught on or caught up. This is one of the great challenges, and opportunities, of our time.

What Is A Company Worth?

A friend of mine has a company that increased its sales from one million dollars to ten million dollars per year over a period of five years and tripled its profits at the same time. Its bank then cut off its line of credit, categorizing the company as a high-risk organization. Why? Because the company had extremely high sales volume but it had not increased its fixed assets- its furniture, fixtures, buildings, cars, computers and so on- at the same speed that it had increased its growth. The bank did not understand that brainpower is the company's primary resource, and that it can be used in an infinite number of ways to create wealth with virtually no investment at all in fixed assets.

Financial institutions today are often baffled at the fact that a hundred million dollar factory can be rendered obsolete by technological change in as little as a year. When a bank today asks for collateral, it has no way of measuring the most valuable assets of the company, the knowledge that exists between the ears of the people who work there. The entire organization could burn to the ground tomorrow but the brainpower could walk across the street and start over again in a few hours.

Just a few decades ago, if a factory burned down, it was out of business. It might never be rebuilt. Sometimes an entire community built around that manufacturing plant would collapse. Today that is no longer the case.

The Winning Edge

The "Winning Edge Concept" is one of the most important ideas of the 20th century. It says that small differences in knowledge and ability can lead to enormous differences in results. Here is an example: if a horse runs in a horse race and comes in first by a nose, it wins ten times as much as the horse that comes in second, by a nose. Does this mean that the horse is ten times faster? Is it twice as fast? 10% as fast? No. The horse is only a nose faster but a nose translates into ten times the prize money.

When a company gets the business in a competitive market, it is often only a tiny bit better than the company that failed to get the business. But the company that wins gets 100% of the sale, 100% of the profit and the salesperson gets 100% of the commission. Is the company or salesperson 100% better than the company or salesperson who loses the deal? No. The company or salesperson has merely developed the "winning edge." And that makes all the difference.

One small piece of information that you have that your competitors lack can be all that it takes for you to gain the winning edge in a particular transaction. An executive said recently, "Our ability to learn and apply new ideas faster than our competition is our only real source of sustainable competitive advantage."

Lifelong Job Security

There is a good deal of talk today about insecurity in the labor force. People are being laid off by the thousands every month, in both good times and bad. This trend will continue, with massive lay-offs every year for the indefinite future. Rapid changes taking place in knowledge and information are creating new products and services, and rendering many current products and services obsolete. When demand shifts, people have to move quickly to jobs producing what customers want today, versus what they wanted yesterday The sum total of human knowledge is doubling every two to three years. This means that you could take all the knowledge accumulated in human history, from every country and in every form, and put it into a huge pile. Three years from now, at most, there would be a pile of new knowledge next to it that is equal to or greater than the first pile.

Knowledge multiplies times itself, which accelerates the development of even more knowledge. A new piece of knowledge can be combined and recombined with other pieces of knowledge to create still more knowledge. Instead of knowledge increasing at a mathematical rate in a steady progression, it is increasing in an exponential rate, faster and faster. By early in the 21st century, the total accumulated knowledge of mankind in certain areas will be doubling every year.

In personal terms, this means that today, your knowledge must double every two to three years just for you to stay even at your current level of ability, at your current income in your current field of work. If your personal knowledge is not increasing at the same speed that general knowledge is increasing in your field, you will be in great danger of becoming obsolete.

The main reason that people are laid off is that companies need new forms of knowledge and skill, and they need more knowledgeable people in newer, more specialized areas. Just as some companies are announcing lay-offs of thousands of people, other companies are hiring thousands of people, in different positions, with different knowledge, performing different tasks.

The Law of Integrative Complexity

The Law of Integrative Complexity explains an important luck factor that can help you to achieve vastly more than the average person. This law states that, "In every group of individuals, the person who can absorb, integrate and apply the greatest quantity of essential information will eventually dominate all the other individuals within that group."

To put it another way, the Law of Integrative Complexity says that the more knowledge and experience you have relative to the particular needs of your organization, the more capable you will be to help the group to succeed and achieve its goals. Power, position, influence and prestige tend to gravitate toward the person who acquires and then uses his or her knowledge the most effectively for the benefit of all.

Knowledge and experience give you the ability to recognize patterns in new situations that arise. The more repeating patterns you can recognize, the faster you can make decisions and take action in any given set of circumstances. The person with the greatest pattern recognition ability will always rise to the top of any organization of value. His or her judgment and contribution will be of greater value and have greater impact on other people and on the results of the organization than anyone else.

Get Ahead and Stay Ahead

For example, the top salespeople tend to remain the top salespeople year after year. Why is this? It is because they have worked many weeks, months and years to become increasingly knowledgeable and skilled at selling ever more of their products or services to ever more sophisticated and demanding customers.

As a result, like runners taking a lead and increasing it as the race goes on, the top salespeople pull ahead, and often way ahead, of their competitors by learning to recognize more and more patterns in more and more complex and varied sales situations. This enables them to identify a potential selling situation quickly. They immediately know what to do and say to get the additional business. As a result, they sell more and more.

With each additional sale, they acquire even more experience. This increased experience, and the patterns that accompany it, enable them to sell even more, easier and faster, in the future. You've heard it said, "Nothing succeeds like success." This is what happens in virtually every competitive field.

Don't Rest On Your Laurels

With the rapid expansion of knowledge in your field, your existing store of knowledge is becoming obsolete at a more rapid rate than ever before. If you were to take a trip around the world in a catamaran and be gone for a year or two, when you got back, you would find that 30%, 40% or even 50% of all the knowledge that you had accumulated that justified your salary and position in your business was no longer valid or of any use any more. You might even have to start over. Your business or industry might no longer exist.

In some fields, the rate of knowledge obsolescence is far faster than in others. For example, the knowledge of a historian or librarian, which are fields that change slowly, may take 10 or 20 years, or even longer to become obsolete. The knowledge of a stockbroker, of prices, market dynamics, interest rates, economic conditions and so on, may become obsolete in a few days, or even hours.

One significant political or economic event can so affect opinion polls as to make all of the accumulated knowledge regarding the outcome of an election obsolete over night, and create a whole new ball game.

The Future Belongs to the Competent

If you want to be lucky, you must never forget that "the future belongs to the competent." The future does not belong to the well meaning, the sincere or the merely ambitious. It belongs to those who are very good at what they do. The future belongs to the people with the critical knowledge of how to get results, and those who are adding to their knowledge base every day.

There is an old saying that, "the rich get richer and the poor get poorer." Today however, it is not a contest today between those who "have more" and those who "have less." It is a competition between those who "know more" and those who "know less." The most significant differences in income in America are between those who are continually increasing their levels of knowledge and skill and those who are not.

To move ahead faster, especially in your financial life, you must remember that: "to earn more, you must learn more." You are maxxed out today at your current level of knowledge and skill. Your "glass ceiling" is within yourself. If you want to increase your income and your earning ability, you have to learn new information, ideas and skills that you can apply to your work to create added value for your company and your customers.

CHAPTER FOUR

MASTERY IS MAGICAL

You have the ability, right now, to exceed all your previous levels of accomplishment. You have within you at this moment the talents you need to be, do and have far more than you have ever achieved in your life to date. This is because you can learn any skills that you need to learn, to do any job you need to do, to achieve any goal that you can set for yourself.

When a violinist plays a perfect piece of classical music in a concert, or when the three tenors — Pavarotti, Domingo and Carrera sing exquisite opera, no one ascribes their accomplishments to luck. When a craftsman builds a beautiful piece of furniture, elegant and refined in every detail, obviously a superb piece of work, no one explains or dismisses his achievement as having been a matter of good luck.

In every case, when you see someone do something in an excellent fashion, you recognize and appreciate a work of mastery. You know that many weeks, months, and even years of hard work and detailed preparation, precede an excellent performance of any kind.

My friend, author of books that have sold in the millions, once told me that many people say his books are easy to read. He said that the reason they were easy to read is because they were so hard to write. Og told me that he would write and rewrite a single paragraph as often as fifteen times so that it flowed smoothly on the page for the reader.

My another good friend, one of the top professional speakers in America, told me that he would often invest as many as one hundred hours of planning, preparation and rehearsal for a one hour talk that he would only give to a single audience on a single occasion.

Business Success Is Not An Accident

When a professional salesperson carefully analyzes his market, identifies his ideal prospects, uses the telephone and fax to set up and confirm appointments, arrives punctually and fully prepared, establishes a high level of rapport, makes an excellent presentation for his product or service and walks away with the order, no one can ascribe his accomplishment to luck. In every case, you are witnessing an example of excellent performance.

There is tremendous resentment against achievement in the world today. In a highly competitive society, it takes many years to become very good at what you do, and to earn the rewards that accrue to top performance. Unfortunately, most people are not willing to make these efforts. Rather than pulling themselves up, they prefer to pull others down. Instead of making progress, they make excuses. They rationalize and justify their poor performance and poor results. The way they do this is by telling you, and others, that you have just been "lucky" while they have, unfortunately, been "unlucky."

But you know the truth. We live in a universe governed by law, not chaos. There is a reason for everything. And great success in any field is largely the result of higher standards and higher overall levels of performance in that field. It has been the same throughout human history and is even truer today in every area of human endeavor.

The Two Metaphors For Success

There are two metaphors for success that are continually used throughout our society: sports and business. In both areas, recognition and rewards go to those individuals and organizations that achieve excellence in competition. We salute and praise those who win in competitive sports. We purchase the products and services of those companies who we feel offer us the very best for the money we pay. In each case, quality and excellence are the measures we use to choose and reward the best performers. It has never been otherwise.

The fact is that the market only pays extraordinary rewards for extraordinary performance. The market pays ordinary rewards for ordinary performance, and below average rewards, unemployment and insecurity for below average performance.

Two Mental Illnesses

There are two mental illnesses that are rampant across America, and much of the industrialized world today. The first is the "something for nothing" disease and the second is the "quick fix" disease. Either of these can sabotage your success but both of them, in combination, can be fatal.

The "something for nothing" disease is contracted by people who think that they can get more out than they put in. They think that they can put in a dollar and get two dollars back. They are constantly looking for opportunities to get something they want without paying full price. They want to go through the revolving door of life on someone else's push.

People with the "something for nothing" disease are trying to violate the basic laws of the universe, the Laws of Sowing and Reaping, Action and Reaction, Cause and Effect. They try to violate one of the great success principles, which is: never attempt to violate universal laws and hope to succeed.

Violating universal laws is the same as attempting to violate the Law of Gravity. You may have heard the story of the person who jumps off a 30-story building to commit suicide. As he falls past the 15th floor, someone leans out of the window and shouts, "How's it going?" The individual, hurling toward the earth, shouts back, "So far, so good!"

Every person who is trying to get out more than they put in is in a similar situation. He may appear to be doing well in the short term, but he is plummeting rapidly toward a rude awakening in life. Don't let this happen to you.

Looking For Short Cuts

The second mental illness is the "quick fix" disease. This is contracted by people who are looking for fast, easy ways to achieve their goals. They look for short cuts to acquire key skills that actually take many months and years of hard work to master. They search for quick ways to solve problems that may have taken them many months or years to develop.

These people become suckers for the latest "get rich quick" idea. They buy lottery tickets and sign up for pyramid schemes. They buy penny stocks and invest in things that they don't know anything about but which promise a quick return. These people often waste many years of hard work and savings searching for the will-o'-the-wisp of quick, easy success.

The Practice of Service

Dedicating yourself to serving others is the way of life that will bring you more luck than you can imagine. The commitment to service helps you to focus on contributing value to those people whose satisfaction determines your own success. The rule is: "Your rewards in life will always be equal to the value of your service to others."

The universe is always in balance. You get out what you put in. If you want to increase the quality and quantity of your rewards, you must focus on increasing the quality and quantity of your service to others.

One of the best questions that you can ask yourself, every single morning, is, "How can I increase the value of my service to my customers today?"

And who are your customers? Your customers are the people who depend upon you for the work that you do. Your customers are those people, the satisfaction of whom determines your rewards, your rate of promotion, your recognition and your progress in your financial and work life.

Identify Your Key Customers

You have more customers than you know. To start with, your boss is your primary customer. Your most important job is to please your boss by doing what he or she considers to be the most important task for you at any given time. If you are a manager, your staff are also your customers. Your job is to please them in such a way that they do an outstanding job in pleasing the people they are meant to serve.

If you are in sales or entrepreneurship, the people in the marketplace who use your products or services are perhaps your most important customers. All great success, all great fortunes, come from serving people with what they want and are willing to pay for better than someone else can serve them.

Deserve the Things You Want

It is a truism in life that, "You do not get what you want but what you deserve." Your central focus on your job is to do whatever is necessary to make sure that you actually deserve the rewards and benefits that you desire. Any attempt to get something that you do not honestly and justly deserve is doomed to failure and frustration. All corrupt or criminal activity, all laziness and corner cutting, is aimed at somehow getting rewards without honestly earning them in the first place.

The word "deserve" comes from the two Latin words, "De" and "Servus." These two words combined mean "From Service."

Many people have the uneasy feeling that they do not deserve to be successful and prosperous. But the truth is that you deserve all the good things that life has to offer as long as you honestly earn them "from service" to others.

Your main concern is to put in the cause, and the effects will take care of themselves. Your job is to put in the seed and nature will give you the harvest. Your goal is to do your work in an excellent fashion. Your rewards will then flow to you as the result of law, not chance.

Do Your Work Well

Dean Briggs of Harvard once wrote, "Do your work. Not just your work, but a little bit more for the lavishing sake. And if you suffer, as you will, do your work. And out of your work and suffering will come the great joys of life."

Peter Drucker once wrote that, even if you are starting a new business off your kitchen table, your goal must be leadership in your industry or you shouldn't even begin at all. If all you want to do is make a quick buck or a little extra income, you will never be particularly successful. You will probably end up losing both your time and your money.

But if your goal is to create a business that offers an excellent product or service, better than anyone else, in a competitive market, and you focus on your goal with tremendous intensity of purpose, you will eventually be a big success in your chosen field. Like Steve Jobs and Steve Wosniak, designing the first Apple computer in a garage, you may end up building a world-class organization.

But even if you don't build a huge company, your commitment to doing your job and serving your customers in an outstanding fashion is the greatest single assurance of your success in the long term.

As an individual, your goal must be to join the top 10% of people in your field. Any goal less than being one of the best is not worthy of you.

Resolve in advance that you will overcome any obstacle, solve any problem and pay any price to be the best at what you do.

Be Prepared To Pay The Price

The achievement of mastery in any field requires months and years of hard work on yourself and your job. Resolve in advance that you will invest whatever time it takes to become excellent at what you do. And be patient. Anything worthwhile takes a long time to accomplish.

I once shared an apartment with a German immigrant who was a master chef. He told me that he was required to study for seven years at the Swiss Culinary Institute in Geneva to become a master chef. He began by learning how to peel fruits and vegetables. He did this for his entire first year until he developed a complete understanding and a deep sensitivity for the texture and feel of fruits and vegetables in all states of freshness, flavor and composition.

In the second year, he moved on to salads and the preparation of fruits and vegetables in simple dishes. In each subsequent year of training, he spent hundreds of hours working with individual spices, sauces, ingredients, and recipes. At the end of seven years, after rigorous testing, he had graduated with perhaps the most respected culinary degree in the world.

He then worked in an internship under a master chef in one of the top restaurants of Europe. After another five years, he was in demand, receiving job offers from all over Europe and America. He was qualified to head up the kitchen of a top hotel or restaurant, if not start his own. The finest hotels and restaurants in the world are those that have been able to attract and hire a graduate of what is called, "The Swiss School." These chefs are highly paid and can eventually retire financially independent.

The point is this: Before they became creative, innovative cooks, such as the famous Wolfgang Puck of Beverly Hills, they had to completely master every part of the culinary art. They had to learn each stage of cooking as it had been learned and passed on over the years by the finest chefs in the world. They did not begin to innovate or change the recipes they were taught before they had reached a very high level of skill and mastery.

Many people in business today think that they can start at the top and work up. They are in a hurry, and cannot be bothered mastering the basics of their jobs. They don't realize that long-term success is the direct result of becoming absolutely excellent at what they do.

Your Attitude Toward Excellence

You can tell if you are in the right field for you by your attitude toward excellence in that field, especially your attitude toward the people who are the very best at what you are doing, or thinking of doing.

All really successful people have great admiration and respect for the top performers in their industries. Since you always move in the direction of what you most admire, the more you look up to and admire the best people in your field, the more you become like them. Make the top people your role models. Compare yourself against the accomplishments of the top people as you evolve and grow.

There are many people working at their jobs who don't particularly care about being at the top of their fields. They are content to be back in the pack, like average runners in a marathon race. They don't really see themselves as capable of winning and they don't particularly care. They are more concerned with security than with achievement.

Even worse, mediocre people often criticize and denigrate the successful people in their industries. They complain about them behind their backs and point out their faults and shortcomings. They get together with other average performers and gossip about the industry leaders, and tell stories. These behaviors are invariably fatal to success. No one who criticizes the high performers in their industry ever becomes a high performer himself.

Attitude Is Everything

The greatest revolution of my generation is the discovery that by changing the inner attitudes of your mind, you can change the outer aspects of your life." (William James)

People are described as lucky when they seem to move ahead faster and go further in a shorter period of time than others. Whenever someone rises to the top of his field and accomplishes wonderful things with his life, people who are not doing as well as he is always ascribe his success to luck.

When you take charge of creating your own future, rather than waiting for it to happen to you, you begin to experience more and more events that the average person dismisses as luck. The main reason that you want to incorporate the principles we are discussing in this book into your life is so that you can have more of the things that you want, faster and easier than you could if you had to spend many years working for them.

Perhaps the most powerful of all luck factors, the one that can make or break you throughout your life, is the quality of your personality, the attitude that you bring to the world and to all of your relationships.

Liking is an essential luck factor. The principle of liking says that, "The more people like you, the more they will be open to your influence and the more they will help you to achieve your goals."

The most popular people tend also to be the most influential people in every field. A positive mental attitude is closely associated with success in almost everything you do. There is an old saying that, "It is not your aptitude but your attitude that determines your altitude." When you become a genuinely positive, optimistic person, people will open doors of opportunity for you that would be closed to most others.

Human beings are predominantly emotional. We decide emotionally and then justify logically. We are almost completely controlled by our feelings, in every situation, and especially in our interactions with others. In a contest between reason and emotion, emotion wins every time.

If you really want to experience a continuous stream of good luck and happy circumstances, you owe it to yourself to develop the kind of personality that radiates warmth and confidence, and which attracts people to you wherever you go. And your true personality is always expressed in your attitude toward others.

The One Thing You Can't Hide

Earl Nightingale called "Attitude" the most important word in the English language, or in any language. Your attitude can be defined as your general emotional approach to any person or situation. It is the one thing about you that people notice immediately. It radiates from you in your facial expression, your tone of voice and your body language. It is seen and felt immediately in every human interaction.

The people around you are affected by your attitude and react almost instantaneously. When you are positive, pleasant and likable with people, they respond by being positive, pleasant and likable right back.

Imagine two people calling on the same business a short time apart. One of them is cheerful, friendly and pleasant. The other one is unsmiling, unhappy and insecure. Which of these two people do you think is going to get past the gatekeeper and get to see the prospective customer?

If you have a choice of buying a product or service, or doing business with two different people, which one would you choose, the positive person or the negative person?

Be A Team Player

At work, the ability to get along well with others, to cooperate and be a good team player, is one of the most admired qualities of the most respected employees. In study after study of turnover in organizations, it has been found that people are usually let go more for their inability to get along with others than for any other reason.

Even in times of recession, it is the negative people who are laid-off first. The positive people, the ones who get along well with everyone, are always the last to go, if they go at all. And if for any reason they are laid-off, they are always the first rehired, either by their previous employer or by someone else.

One of the ways to assure that you have a great life is for you to be liked and appreciated by everyone with whom you work. You will get more opportunities and steadier promotions. You will be paid more money and be given greater responsibilities. As a result of your positive mental attitude, the people around, above, and below you, and at your same level, will want you to succeed and will do everything possible to help you.

A person with a positive attitude can make more progress in a couple of years than a person with a negative attitude could make in ten or twenty years. We all like to buy from and work with people who are pleasant and who make us feel good about ourselves when we are around them. And your words and behavior are very much under your own control.

Perhaps the most important step you ever take is to take full control of your words and actions, and make sure that everything you do is helping you. Resolve every day to behave like the kind of person you want to be thought of and spoken about by other people.

The Key To Your Personality

Your self-esteem is the key to your personality. How you genuinely feel about yourself determines your impact on others more than any other factor. Your self-esteem is best defined as, "how much you like yourself." The more you like and respect yourself, the more you will like and respect others, and the more they will like and respect you. Everything you do and say to build and reinforce your own self esteem improves your attitude and your relationships with other people.

This is another way of saying again that your outer world will be a reflection of your inner world. Your outer world of relationships will be a reflection of your inner world of personal worth and value.

Mental fitness is very much like physical fitness. They both require regular training. And just as you become physically fit by exercising your body, you become mentally fit by exercising your mind. You build your physical muscles by working on them continuously. You build your mental muscles, your levels of self-esteem, self-respect and self-confidence, by working on them in specific ways as well.

You eat healthy, nutritious foods every day to nourish and sustain high levels of physical health and energy. In the same way, you feed your mind with healthy mental foods every day to keep yourself cheerful, optimistic and upbeat, no matter what happens.

Your Mental Fitness Program

We have already talked about many of the exercises in your mental fitness program. Let's review some of them one more time:

First, to eliminate the negative emotions of anger, blame, envy, resentment and self-pity, you make a conscious decision to accept complete responsibility for your life, for everything you are and everything you will ever be. You refuse to make excuses or to blame anyone else. You see yourself as the primary creative force in your own present and your own future. You realize that you are where you are and what you are because of your own choices and decisions in the past, and since you made those choices and decisions, only you are responsible.

Second, you take charge of your life by seeing yourself as active rather than passive. You make things happen rather than waiting and hoping for them to happen. You see yourself as a master of change rather than as a victim of change. You "never complain, never explain." If you are not happy with some part of your life, you get busy and do something about it. But you refuse to allow negative emotions to interfere with your personality or to cloud your vision.

Third, you set clear, written goals for yourself in each important area of your life. You create written plans of action to achieve them. You work on your major goals every day. You maintain a sense of forward momentum and progress that gives you energy and enthusiasm. You keep yourself so busy working on things that are important to you that you don't have time to be worry about little irritations, or situations that are out of your control.

This dynamite combination of accepting complete responsibility and then designing a clear written plan for your life gives you a foundation upon which you can build as high as you want to go. These two actions give you a tremendous sense of personal power and enable you to create your own future.

Fourth, you recognize that knowledge and skill are the keys to financial freedom. The more you learn, the more you earn. The more you learn about your field, the more opportunities you will have to use your increasing knowledge. You work on becoming better every day. You know that, "If you're not getting better, you're getting worse."

Fifth, you recognize that personal mastery in your field is absolutely essential to success, achievement and what people call "luck." Excellent performance opens every door, and is the key to your earning what you are really worth.

Sixth, you have a plan for personal and professional development that includes reading, listening to audio programs, attending courses and seminars and taking every opportunity to increase your knowledge and skill. The more you work on becoming better at the key skills you need to achieve your goals, the more confident and competent you feel. You know that success is not an accident. Luck is just a word that people use to explain the good things that continually happen to people who are excellent at what they do.

Seventh, and perhaps most important of all, you know that you become what you think about, most of the time. You therefore discipline yourself to think continually about the things that you want, and keep your mind off of the things you don't want.

Program Your Mind For Success

There are a series of powerful mental programming techniques that you can use throughout the day to become a more positive and effective person. Each of these techniques is both practical and proven, and the combination of all of them together can make you both irresistible and unstoppable.

The first of these techniques is the regular use of positive affirmations to program your subconscious mind, and to keep yourself feeling optimistic and upbeat throughout the day. Fully 95% of your emotions are determined by your "self talk," by the way you talk to yourself moment to moment. By controlling and directing your inner dialogue, you take control of your thoughts, feelings and actions, and ultimately, your own future.

Dr. Martin Seligman of the University of Pennsylvania calls this your "Explanatory Style." The way that you talk to yourself and explain things to yourself largely determines how you feel about your what is going on around you. In other words, it is not what happens to you, but how you interpret what happens to you, that determines your response, positive or negative.

If you do not consciously and deliberately think and talk about the things you want, you have a natural tendency to begin thinking about the things that you don't want to happen, the people or situations that make you upset or angry. If you do not firmly take control of your own mind, and keep your thoughts focused on where you want to go, you will, by default, slip into the negativity and worry that is common to most people.

The principle of affirmation says that, "Strong, affirmative statements repeated continually in your conscious mind will inevitably be accepted as commands by your subconscious mind."

Whatever goal or command you program into your subconscious mind will begin to materialize in the world around you. A new goal activates your reticular activating system. This increases your awareness and sensitivity to people, ideas and opportunities that can help you. It enables you to put your foot on the accelerator of your own potential and move more rapidly towards your goals.

Positive self-talk and positive affirmations are the tools you use to control your thinking and keep focused on achieving your goals. With positive affirmations, your potential is unlimited. You can literally talk yourself into becoming the kind of person that you want to be. The most powerful words in the world are the words that you say to yourself and believe.

The best all purpose affirmation you can use to build your self-esteem and self-confidence are the words, "I like myself! I like myself! I like myself!" over and over.

When you first say, "I like myself!" you may feel a bit uneasy or uncomfortable inside. You may feel that the words are phony. This is quite normal. Psychologists refer to this feeling as cognitive dissonance. You experience it whenever a new, positive message you are affirming clashes with an old negative message stored in your subconscious as the result of unhappy experiences in your past.

But when you repeat the positive affirmation, "I like myself!" over and over, eventually your subconscious mind accepts these words as your new operating instructions. You begin to feel, think and then act like a person with high self-esteem. The more you like yourself, the more you like others. You become a more positive person. And the more you like others, the more they like you and want to cooperate with you. It begins with your own self-esteem.

Another powerful affirmation you can use is the words, "I'm the best! I'm the best! I'm the best!" repeated over and over. Whenever you think of yourself and your work, tell yourself, in strong, positive terms that you are the best, and getting better. Tell yourself that you are excellent at what you do. Again, you may feel a little strange when you first start saying this to yourself, but after a short while, you will feel more and more comfortable with this new message. And it will start to be true. Your performance will improve day by day.

A wonderful way to use affirmations is for you to start off every day by repeating the words, "I feel happy, I feel healthy, I feel terrific!"

When people ask you how things are going, always reply positively by saying, "Great!" Or, "Wonderful!"

Talk about yourself and your life the way you want them to be, not the way they might happen to be at the moment. Remember, before you can experience it in your reality, you must convince your subconscious mind that you already have it. If you don't feel positive and enthusiastic at the moment, pretend that you do. "Fake it until you make it."

CHAPTER FIVE

RELATIONSHIPS ARE ESSENTIAL

"The best portion of a good man's life, - his little nameless, unremembered acts of kindness and of love." (William Wordsworth)

The quality and quantity of your relationships with other people will determine your success as much or more than any other factor. In the last chapter, you learned several ways to become a far more, positive, optimistic and likable person. In this chapter, you will learn how to systematically expand your network of contacts and relationships. This strategy will help you increase the likelihood that you will meet the right person at the right time with the right information or opportunity for you.

The Law of Relationships explains one of the most critical success factors of all. It says, "Relationships are essential; the more people who know you and think of you in a positive way, the more opportunities you will have to achieve your goals."

Every important change in your life will involve other people. If you want to achieve big goals, you will need the active involvement and cooperation of many other people. Often, the direction of your life will be changed by a simple comment, a piece of advice or a single action by one person. The more good relationships you have, and the more helpful people you know, the more often the right doors will open for you.

The Law Of Relationships In Action

A friend of mine was growing his business in an extremely competitive market. He needed more money to expand. He began calling on local banks with his business plan. One by one, they turned him down and told him that his business would never be successful.

But he was an optimist. He drew a series of ever expanding concentric circles around the address and location of his business and began calling on banks at ever-greater distances. Finally, he found a bank and a banker 95 miles away who liked his business plan and loaned him the money he needed to expand. He is today one of the wealthiest and most successful entrepreneurs in America.

I asked him if he had ever thought about giving up his search for the money he needed. He said, "Absolutely not! I knew that I would eventually get the money if I spoke to enough people. I was prepared to visit banks even 500 miles from my office if that's what it took to find the right banker with the right attitude for what I needed."

Improve the Odds In Your Favor

This is a key luck factor and an important part of success. Remember the Law of Probabilities, which says, "The more different things you try, the more likely it will be that you will try the right thing at the right time."

This law applies to relationships as well. The more people you know, and the more consistently you expand your range of contacts, the more likely it is that you will meet the person you need, at exactly the right time, with exactly the right resources for you. When it happens, as it always does, it will not be a miracle, and it will have nothing to do with luck.

The most successful people in our society, at all levels, are those who know, and who are known by, the greatest number of other successful people. But this is very much a chicken and egg situation. Do people become successful and then meet other successful people? Or do they meet other successful people, and then become successful themselves?

The fact is that it can work either way. One mistake that many people make is that they think that by getting around other successful people, they will be able to piggyback on their knowledge, advice and resources. This however will only work for a short time. In the long run, you can never get and hold on to anything to which you are not entitled to as the result of your own accomplishments, talents and personality.

Focus On Attracting Key People

The Law of Attraction is perhaps the most important of the luck factors. "You inevitably attract into your life the people and circumstances in harmony with your dominant thoughts."

The opposite of the Law of Attraction is the Law of Repulsion, which says, "You automatically drive away or repel people and circumstances that are not in harmony with your dominant thoughts."

When you think positively most of the time, you set up a force field of positive energy that attracts other positive people and situations toward you. If you think negatively, you set up a field of negative energy that drives these same forces away.

Birds of a feather do flock together. People at similar levels of success in every enterprise or profession tend to be attracted to each other. And you cannot fake it for very long.

Implement the Law of Indirect Effort

This brings us to an important luck factor — the Law of Indirect Effort. This law says that you get what you want with other people more often indirectly than directly. In fact, if you attempt to get other people to help you or cooperate with you directly, you will often end up looking foolish. You will actually drive those people away.

But if you use the Law of Indirect Effort, you will be amazed at how successful you can be. For example, if you want to have more friends, how do you use the Law of Indirect Effort? It's simple. Concentrate on being a good friend to others. Take an interest in them. Ask them questions and listen to what they have to say. Be empathetic. Express interest and concern about their problems and their situations. Look for ways to help them, even if it is just by being a friendly sounding board. The more you concentrate on being a good friend, the more friends you will have. You will attract people into your life like bees to honey.

Do you want to impress other people? The worst way to do it is the direct way, by trying to impress them. The best way is the indirect way, by being impressed by other people. The more impressed you are with other people and their accomplishments, the more interested and impressed they will be with you and yours. Everyone has done something that is noteworthy and impressive. When you meet a new person, your job is to find it out.

Ask people what they do. Ask people how they got into their particular field. Ask people how everything is going in their business. If you listen carefully, people will tell you about both their current successes and their current problems. When a person mentions that they have just achieved something worthwhile, be sure to congratulate them.

Everybody Likes A Compliment

Abraham Lincoln once said, "Everybody likes a compliment." People love to be acknowledged and admired for things they have accomplished. Make it a policy to find out what they have achieved and then compliment them on their successes.

A successful businessman I know made a habit of sending ten telegrams every week to people he had met over the years. The telegrams contained a single word, "Congratulations!"

Over the years he built up a wide network of men and women who liked and respected him. They were always amazed that he had somehow known that they had accomplished something worthwhile and had acknowledged them with his telegram.

When he was asked, later on in life, how he managed to be aware of the accomplishments of so many of his friends, he said that he had had no idea what they were doing. He just knew that everybody is accomplishing something every day, and every week. When you send them a message that says "Congratulations!" they will automatically apply that message to whatever situation in their life that has just worked out successfully for them.

By using the Law of Indirect Effort, you constantly look for ways to compliment and congratulate people on what they are doing, what they have accomplished, how they are dressed, the recent decisions they have made, or even the fact that they have lost a few pounds.

In our society, one of the best compliments that you can give to anyone is, "You look like you've lost weight!" Even if it's not true, people always enjoy having someone notice, rightly or wrongly, that they have lost weight. Why? Because everyone wants to be physically attractive, and physical attractiveness is closely associated with being thin, trim and fit. You can never go wrong complimenting someone on how good they look.

Satisfy One of the Deepest Human Needs

Do you want people to respect you? This is one of the deepest of all needs. Almost everything you do is to earn the respect of the people you respect, or at least not to lose the respect of the people you respect. So if you want people to respect you, the best way is for you to respect them, in advance.

We have moved away from the era of the "go-getter" and we are now in the era of the "go-giver." Successful people are always looking for ways to do things for other people. The great majority of under achievers and unhappy people are those who are waiting for others to do something for them, in advance. They want to get something out before they put something in.

But this attitude violates the Law of Sowing and Reaping. You cannot reap until you have sown. You therefore concentrate on sowing good thoughts, good ideas and good feelings in your relationships with others. You know, as a matter of universal law, that these same things will come back to you in the most remarkable ways.

Give Generously of Yourself

The Law of Giving, another key luck factor, says "the more you give of yourself without expectation of return, the more that will come back to you from the most unexpected sources."

Many people make the mistake of thinking that their good should come back to them from the very people that they have been good to. But this very seldom happens. When you give generously to someone else, either of your time, money or emotion, that person will very seldom be the person who repays you in kind. Instead, you will be activating one of the great laws of the universe, the law of attraction, and powers will be put in motion that will bring you the good that you need and desire, usually from a completely different source, and at exactly the right time and place for you.

Why should this happen? It's easy to understand. When you do something nice for another person, it raises your own self-esteem and makes you feel better about yourself. This heightened feeling of positive energy activates your powers of attraction. You become a more powerful magnet for people and circumstances consistent with your goals. Good things start to happen to you.

There is something about helping others, about giving of yourself to others in need, that makes you wonderful about yourself. In fact, you are designed in such a way that you can only be truly happy when you know that you are doing something that makes a positive difference in the lives of other people.

The reality is that you benefit as much, and often, much more, than the person for whom you do a kindness. You change the force field of mental energy around you by helping others in some way. You intensify the power of attraction and draw into your life helpful people and circumstances from sources that you could not imagine or predict.

Activate the Principle of Serendipity

Serendipity works in strange ways. Here is an example. Imagine you are driving from Point A to Point B. You are in a hurry but you see an old person who is stopped by the side of the road with a flat tire. Even though you are on a tight schedule, you overcome your impatience and stop your car to help the elderly man replace his tire. He offers to pay you but you refuse. You wish him a pleasant journey and you hurry on toward your destination. The whole incident takes about ten minutes.

Perhaps unbeknownst to you, you have just activated the powers of the universe in your behalf. You arrive at your appointment a little bit late, but you find that the person you are going to meet is even later than you. Nothing is lost. Not only that, something has happened that morning and the person you meet with, rather than being a reluctant prospect, is very much in need of what you are selling and makes an immediate decision to buy. You walk out with one of the best and easiest orders you've ever recieved, and if you're not careful, you will start thinking about how "lucky" you were. But it wasn't luck. It was law.

Generosity of all kinds triggers happy, serendipitous events in your life. Throughout the ages, many men and women have tithed their way to great success and fortune. They have regularly given 10% or more of their income to worthy causes. This attitude of generosity and the action of giving seems to set up a force field of energy that drew financial opportunities to them that were far greater than any money they give away.

Generosity Really Pays

John D. Rockefeller began his life as a clerk earning $3.75 per week. He saved 20% of his income and gave 50% to his church. He lived on the remaining 30%. Eventually, he got into the fledgling oil business and built Standard Oil, the biggest oil company in the United States.

There is an interesting sequel to the John D. Rockefeller story. His entire fortune was based on his obsessive drive to reduce the cost of fuel oil to the American consumer. He used every business strategy possible to acquire ever-greater quantities of gas and oil. He built complex and sophisticated systems of distribution and delivery. He was so efficient that he was able to continually lower fuel prices. He was able to take away the market from anyone who was charging more than he was. His company, Standard Oil, was called a monopoly, but it was completely customer centered. It was built on his ability to give his customers what they wanted cheaper than anyone else.

As his business interests grew and expanded, he lost sight of his original desire to share his benefits with others. In the back of his mind, he had always intended to give money to worthy causes, but he became so busy building his empire that he simply didn't have the time.

When Rockefeller was 52 years old, he was the richest man in the world. He was also a physical wreck. He was in a state of collapse. His body was falling apart. The doctors told him that he only had a few months, perhaps a year, to live. He had worked for so long, and so hard, and had taken such poor care of himself physically, that even though he could afford any kind of treatment, there was nothing they could do for him,

Rockefeller decided that if he was going to die anyway, he was going to go back to his original intention and give away some of his money. He sold half of his interests in the Rockefeller oil companies for cash, an amount of about $500 million dollars. He then set up the first Rockefeller Foundation and began giving his money away to worthy causes that he had admired over the years. And a remarkable thing happened. The more money he gave away, the healthier he became.

Eventually, his physical problems cleared up. The more dedicated he became to charitable causes, to funding churches and foundations and other needy organizations, the better he felt, and the healthier, happier and more positive he became.

Meanwhile, the Rockefeller oil companies continued to grow. The half ownership that he retained in his companies increased in value at a rate faster than he could give the other half away. Rockefeller lived to the age of 92, another forty years. By the time he died, he had given away hundreds of millions of dollars. But the incredible thing was that he was worth more when he died than when he had sold half of his interests at the age of 52 and began his charitable activities.

The Giver Benefits More Than the Receiver

Many of the great family fortunes of the world are characterized by generosity and altruism. It seems that the more you give away of your wealth, without anyone knowing, and with no expectation of return, the more you activate the powers of the universe to work on your behalf.

CONCLUSION

One-third of all Americans are dissatisfied with the future facing themselves and their families, according to a recent Gallup survey. And even among those who are satisfied, their optimism about the future is the lowest it's been in 40 years.

 The good news: you can create your own future. Better yet, you can do it simply and systematically as part of your everyday life, inside and outside the workplace.

Don't leave your future to chance or fate, or to the whims of others. Instead, unlock and live your best future, beginning in the here and now.

Printed in Great Britain
by Amazon